Intro

"I can't believe this guy is back here again!" I remark as I pull into the parking lot. It's the fifth day this week I've seen him perpetuate this ingenious scam. It's a work of art with its perfect timing, simplicity and flawless execution. At least a few times a week this older gentlemen, who bears a striking resemblance to Super Mario, that is, if Mario were out on Workman's Comp after suffering a Princess-saving related injury. This gentleman convinces strangers that he needs a few dollars to go see his doctor. Some people flat out rebuke him at first sight, but he's so tenacious, and so convincing, that most hand him a few bucks or some change. Then, in a brilliant stroke of master genius, he takes said money, crosses the parking lot to the bus stop and acts like he's waiting to get on the bus. Once he notices that the Good Samaritan has departed, he resumes his position in the lot and repeats the whole process at least ten more times. It's like he's level and gold grinding in some weird Delco Role Playing Game. I don't know his name but I call him Charon the Ferryman because he's literally going back and forth over a sea of blacktop. I always give him a few coins when I see him so he doesn't waste time telling me his elaborate tale. I'd be lying if I said I wasn't impressed. It definitely doesn't shock me, this being the Wawa parking lot and all. The normal rules of the world don't apply here.

You may have just asked, "What the hell is a Wawa?" Those who aren't in the know often do. Well, it's the most magical place in the world. It had its beginnings as a dairy farm that delivered milk to homes in Pennsylvania and New Jersey. It grew to become a regional convenience store when supermarkets found the need for milk delivery obsolete and fathers grew tired of their children belonging to the milkman. What started with one store has now grown to 720 stores in six states that employ 23,000 people, all spreading the gospel of the hoagie. A convenience store for people who hate to be inconvenienced, the store offers a variety of prepared foods, snacks, drinks, toilet paper, gas, and acts as sort of a Statue Of Liberty in the Philly area: "Give me your tired, your stoned, your drunk masses."

Out late and need something to soak up all that booze? Wawa has a hoagie for that. Work the late shift and need a hot cup of coffee because your kids wouldn't let you sleep during the day? Wawa has you covered. Need to feed the kids in between an exhausting marathon of organized events they all participate in? Wawa has some of the best and freshest foods available. From prepared salads to bags of chips, they have you covered. Wawa is open 24/7 and there for you, unlike your emotionally unavailable father. This is why it inspires an ISIS-like fanaticism in its customers who would wage jihad tomorrow, if the stores were to shutter.

In a world that is often chaotic, Wawa offers a brief respite. It is familiar and consistent. Every store is laid out in a similar fashion and each prepared food item (made by an equally consistent and helpful staff) tastes the same, no matter if you're in a store in Philly, Jersey, Delaware, Virginia and now Florida. The store welcomes you in a way that your warm, favorite, cardigan-loving uncle would welcome you into his home on a cold, rainy day. Consistency is what drives people to trudge through their mundane lives to this store. The promise of a good meatball sandwich or a milkshake when the burdens of life become too great is enough to make people drive to the ends of the earth to reach a Wawa. If other food joints are a desert, then Wawa is an oasis.

Yet, the consistency isn't just limited to their product, it also extends to their customer base. And that base shows it's true colors in the parking lot.

The Wawa parking lot is reminiscent of the cantina scene in "Star Wars". It's filled with all sorts of strange and weird people who look like demons and aliens, and if you steal the parking spot of a roofer you may just lose an arm.

They are hell to navigate. There are various people pulling in and out, their hands filled with food or hot coffees or cold ICEEs. The scene is often a melee of pedestrians with angry scowls weaving in and out of cars coupled with divorced parents swapping children while screaming at each other, secret lovers switching cars to head off to some tryst and usually someone arguing. Frat bros in ten-gallon hats buying bags of ice on their way to a concert, treating the parking lot like it's the quad from their college days. You can see children on bikes weaving dangerously through the parking lot while holding fistfuls of candy. It's frenetic, loud and it can be disorienting and overwhelming if you linger too long. The only calming presence in the parking lot are the gargoyles of Wawa. That's the old men you see congregating by the trash can. They are the first things you will notice even before you find a parking spot.

Normally, one would not stand next to a garbage can, but these trash cans double as a makeshift meeting place, a coffee table, or a lunch counter. Most times, you will find someone unraveling a Sizzli breakfast sandwich or hoagie on top of the can, treating it the same way they would a kitchen table. Most of the time you'll find a gaggle of old men gathered around the trashcan, their coffee and Marlboro Reds sitting comfortably on top. These men are usually decked out in accoutrement from their military days. Others come dressed in construction overalls, some just in LL Bean. From different walks of life, bound by their love of decent affordable coffee and cigarettes that pair so well with it, they set up camp on a daily basis.

It's a secret, boys-only club. I have never been asked to join. They don't just let anyone in. I assume you've either got to be retired or active military, or wearing paint-splattered pants. What they talk about is a mystery to everyone. They guard the space around the trash can like it's some holy relic from the Crusades and when an outsider enters to use the can for its intended purpose they clam up like pinched mobsters.

I walk past them and think, perhaps they are the gatekeepers. The St. Peter's guardians of some secret knowledge. Most likely, they are just a bunch of retired guys who probably don't want to be home with their wives. Nevertheless, they bookend most Wawa stores. They are the first and last things you see when you visit the store. Maybe they are the keepers of the sacred codes of the **"Fast Flying Goose,"** the true spirit of Wawa.

Wawa instills a deep loyalty and honor in its customers. This loyalty is never more on display than in the concept of holding the door. If you've never seen it then it probably comes across as some weird land-based trapeze act, but there's poetry and honor in this act. I've seen people damn near fight one another over a parking spot only to apologize and hold the door for one another while entering. To not hold the door for either an incoming or outgoing customer is akin to insulting their mother. It goes against the utilitarian spirit of both the store and the customers who frequent it. You don't kick grandma and you always hold the door at Wawa. A vestige left over perhaps from a more civilized and polite time or as my friend Dave once said, "Maybe people hold the door for one another because on some level everyone realizes just how bad life sucks."

If life were awful, then the parking lot would be Hell and Wawa itself, purgatory. Every trip you take there would be like you are living out Dante's Inferno. Instead of horrors unimaginable and being forced to abandon all hope when you enter, you'd meet the same five types of people with the opportunity to grab a sandwich while you're there. This is what Wawa is, and these are the people who call it their favorite store. And as I hold the door for the customer behind me, I take all of these things into consideration as if instead of buying lunch, I am being quizzed.

The Girl In Pajamas

I always laugh when I exit the vestibule and enter into Wawa proper. As I glide past the newspaper rack I watch as an old man comfortably reads The Daily Times. It reminds me that most people treat the store like it's an extension of their own home. Wawa has no written dress code aside from the typical "No Shoes, No Shirt, No Service" but it might as well be labeled "Pajama Casual", due to the massive amount of clientele wearing pajama bottoms. I look around and realize that at any given time, the pajama-clad people make it impossible to discern if the store is having some sort of promotional sleepover. Once relegated to the bedroom or those suffering an emotionally devastating breakup, pajamas have become haute couture for a certain subset of the Wawa clientele. The PJ Clan wants all of the comfort of being on their couch, without the shame associated with your life falling apart. I scan the crowd and the people wearing pajamas are too numerous to count. I laugh thinking that once upon a time we used to get dressed up to fly in an airplane. I mean how else do you get bumped to first class?

The PJ Clan is now a universal truth, just as the sun rising in the east, setting in the west, time always flowing forward and the Eagles never winning a Super Bowl, there will always be a girl in Wawa wearing pajamas.

As I move toward the cold drinks case, which is the length of a wall, I pass a grown man in his fifties wearing pajama pants and an Eagles jersey. I think he woke up late for the game and forgot to change before heading to the stadium. Yes, men are guilty of this same sartorial faux pas, yet it is most prevalent amongst women ages 13 to you should know better.

I turn to see a young woman walk through the door wearing a clean pair of pajamas with her hair and makeup immaculately done. She is so pretty you'd half expect her to pause and wave because she looks like she's the prom queen in a teen movie. Bumping directly into her is another young woman, as pretty but seemingly holding back tears, clearly the runner-up. She races straight past the prom queen toward the ATM, and I strain to hear her sniffle. I imagine what's going on without staring too much. Perhaps she's reeling from a bad breakup, or death in the family, or a fate-sealing pregnancy test. I don't know. I'll probably never know. She's gone just as fast as she came, and on the edge of a full-on emotional meltdown by the time she exits. The old men by the trash can just stare at her as she goes by, saying nothing.

She disappears from sight and I turn to the mountains upon mountains of Doritos and Lay's potato chips, toward the endless bank of reach-in coolers holding the drinks. The variety of choices is vast. From Gatorade to Wawa-specialty drinks to a machine that dispenses every soda imaginable it feels as overwhelming as asking a girl out on a date.

As I'm zeroing in on selecting a Pepsi, I hear a loud shriek from the other end of the aisle that can only be described as the sound a raccoon makes when you shoot it with a BB gun. A short brunette with pale skin reminiscent of a white walker from "Game of Thrones" is screaming into her cellphone. Holding it ever so slightly from her mouth like it's a microphone, her hair looks like it was washed with bacon grease, flops all around her gaunt face as she screams "No, no NO!" over and over again like it's a refrain in a hit song. The oversized legs of her My Little Pony pajama pants are coal-miner's-lung black from having been dragged through so many dirty parking lots and dusty stores. Her poorly drawn, possibly received in prison neck and wrist tattoos jut out of her stained Gap sweatshirt, like pictures in a pop-up book anytime she emphatically makes a point.

I can't make out what she's screaming about as the sound of a child being scolded by an employee is drowning her out, but I've seen this play out before a thousand times in thousands of different Wawas. Usually it's about some other girl talking crap about her or another perceived slight, or how her baby daddy isn't paying child support. She's walking toward me while still screaming into her phone blissfully unaware that I and everyone within earshot now knows that her boyfriend got locked up for selling Percocet. I've overheard so many of these conversations and I've learned so much about custody rights, parole violations, and visitation, that I feel like I could have a future as a court-appointed mediator.

It now feels like a duel, as she's slowly walking toward me and I toward her. We're hemmed in, surrounded by the cold drinks in the cooler and the cases and liters of soft drinks on our right. If she pulled a gun and were to start shooting this whole place would erupt like those videos you see on YouTube of people putting Mentos in soda bottles.

I open the cooler door to reach for a Pepsi just as I hear her scream "Go to hell" into her phone and she barely avoids getting hit in the face with the door.

"Excuse me, I'm sorry." I say as I try to be both polite, yet not engaging enough to welcome a personal attack.

"It's cool," she says as she pushes between me and the cooler door. I try not to wince at the paranoid thought that her simply walking by may have just exposed me to bed bugs, scabies, or worse.

Her smile looks like a jack-o-lantern smile as she grabs a Mountain Dew and slides out of the way of the closing door.

For a split-second our eyes catch. Underneath her mud-brown irises are bags that speak more of the bad choices she's made in her life and less about sleep or vitamin deficiency. I panic as our eyes have now locked on more than is usually appropriate and I blurt out "Is everything ok? I heard you screaming on your phone" instantly knowing it was a mistake.

She recoils in horror as if I just asked her to join me in an orgy with the Wawa guardians behind the store in the dumpster, even though it looks like that's where she may have gotten her outfit.

"That's none of your damn business, dude." She fires back. Technically she's right, it is none of my business and it takes the strength of God for me not to scream, "Well if you didn't broadcast it to the entire store then maybe I wouldn't want to know when Bobby is getting out of jail!" But I don't. I look down and reply "Fair enough."

She cocks her head back and instantly transforms from a down-on-her-luck woman of dubious employment and a possible drug problem to full-on Gollum seeking his Precious and screams "Maybe if you spent less time worrying about other people's business you wouldn't be dressed up like some glorified paperboy!"

She is now inches away from me and her scent is a mixture of unwashed laundry and cigarettes. So pungent is this smell and so angry her tone and posture that it literally pushes me back up against the soda display.

I put my hands up in a sign of both surrender and protection and mutter "Look I was just trying to be sympathetic. I didn't mean to intrude. I've had some bad days in my life."

A confused look washes over her face, like why would I even care about her or her problems at all. Her lips tremble and she says "Unless you can get my man out of jail then there's nothing you can do for me." Her eyes well up with tears. One slowly makes its way down her cheek. Color returns to her face and just as she raises her arm to unleash a thousand wrongs and disappointments upon me a tiny voice calls out, "Mommy, can I get this?"

We both whip our heads to the top of the aisle and look at this tiny child, maybe all of four, holding a KitKat bar. I can't determine the sex of the child due to the short, unkempt hair, and the mosaic of dirt and food coloring on its face. Left unattended to roam the aisles while its mother dealt with the latest in a series of crises.

The mother shouts, "NO!" and snaps out of her near breakdown as if she was a robot who was suddenly switched on. "PUT THAT BACK RIGHT NOW!"

She marches toward the child and yanks the candy bar out of the kid's hand. She then grabs it and begins to pull it out of the aisle. The child looks up at her and asks, "Mommy, who was that?" and she looks back toward me and responds, "Some dickhead who needs to mind his own business."

I watch her drag her kid off. I put away the soda and decide perhaps I'll have a coffee instead.

Cops

As I stroll past the endless display of diabetes-inducing soft drinks, wanting to shake off that interaction and its smell, I'm nearly run over by a young looking police officer. He swings open the cooler door with the force of a hurricane, nearly tearing it off the hinges like it was a weak screen door. He quickly grabs a fistful of Monster Energy drinks as if he's waging a war on his kidneys instead of crime. As he flies past me I think of how the Bangles lied to us in their song, "Walk Like An Egyptian" because I've never once seen a cop eat a doughnut or in a doughnut shop. As a matter of fact, I've never seen a cop eat a doughnut. The Bangles and Big Doughnut must be perpetuating that myth.

I have seen cops in Wawa. They're there every time I step foot in one, which is usually four times a day due to my crippling addiction to both coffee and cigarettes. Today is no different. As I approach, the coffee station is set up like the pit crews at The Daytona 500. Instead of tires, there are endless flavors of coffee, creamers and sugar. There are also two older cops camped out as if they were assigned to guard the pumpkin spice coffee from rabid white 30 somethings.

The young cop who buzzed by me has no time to linger and chew the fat. He's got a world to save. These two older cops have long since accepted that their job is a Sisyphean endeavor. You remove a drug dealer from the corner today, another pops up tomorrow, and so on and so forth. It's almost like they understand that their job is a realistic portrayal of the movie, "Groundhog's Day", but with guns and moving violations.

This idea of repetition becomes ever more present on the one balding cop's face. I grab a 20 ounce coffee cup and look over at him as he takes a sip from his coffee and does that "A thousand domestic disputes" stare into the ether like he's replaying a classic epic Greek tragedy in his mind.

These cops look exactly like all the other cops: the uniform, the walkie-talkie on their shoulders, the backbreaking utility belt with nightstick, taser and firearm, the catholic schoolboy haircuts they wear are high and tight and the badge that is more often than not a target of fear and derision.

From behind me I hear a construction worker moan, "Damn cops get free coffee. Must be nice." With such a condescending and judgmental tone that he doesn't even take into account the symbiotic relationship between cops and Wawa. Their presence makes it so my drunken ass can purchase condoms at 2 a.m. without fear of catching a bullet in the back of my head during a robbery. I am fairly confident that if I were face down on the floor I wouldn't be thinking "Screw those guys and the free coffee!" Nope. I would be whimpering, "Oh my god please kill the bad guys! I haven't finished season three of *Breaking Bad* yet."

As I stare at the officers a little too long, I can't help but think how societal opinion has changed. We've gone from "Officer Friendly" who visited you in school to tools of the police state who are hell bent on bullying the public. As I scan the wrinkles in their faces, it's difficult for me to imagine what it's like to be under that kind of scrutiny while dealing with the worst that society has to offer, in addition to having a schedule that is conducive to and makes them think that their spouses are running around on them. One by one, people give them icy stares and it really surprises me that more cops don't pull a Yosemite Sam and start licking off shots in all directions. I know I would, if my job consisted of going from zero to murder, to traffic stop, and then back again. I keep this in mind as I approach to fill up my coffee.

"Hello, officers." I say as I fill up my coffee. I'm nervous the same way I would be if I were to ask for one of their daughter's hand in marriage.

"Hey there." The balding cop says as the clean-cut cop with the salt and pepper hair nods in my direction. Cordial but not overly chatty, I assume it's less to do with their personality and more of a reaction to a society that has grown hostile to their very being.

I laugh out loud recalling a football game where I once saw how the cops had an awful go of tackling a naked guy on the field and I asked, "Officers, is it really that hard to tackle a naked guy? I see it on TV all the time." I'm generally curious and partly trying to make them laugh.

Without hesitation the balding cop arches his brow, leans in and says in a matter of fact tone, "Try catching one high on meth."

"No way! It's that hard??" I immediately respond, high off of the response I got.

"Oh man." The other cop says as he pivots my way, "It's like trying to catch a greased up pig who wants to bite you and won't stop rambling on about lizard robot people."

We all begin to laugh together. Emboldened by the laughter I was able to get, I asked, "Can I ask another stupid question?" feeling that I've earned their trust now that I've proven I'm not some guy who's complaining about a parking ticket.

"Fire away," the balding cop says, clearly the more talkative of this Punch and Judy duo.

"Do you guys call criminals perps?"

They look at each other and make a face that's part sarcastic, part sick of this question.

"Hell no. This isn't Blue Bloods. Cops don't talk that way at all. What the public seems to think of our job due to TV and the reality are so far off it's unreal. They don't make shows about what our jobs are really like."

Now I'm super curious so I asked ,"So what would that show look like?"

"Well it would be about cops sitting in their cars for hours on end with the occasional noise complaint or traffic violation. Maybe there would be a domestic dispute. Pepper in some coffee drinking. A lot less guns and way more aimless driving and telling teenagers to go home. They make a show like that and it would be cancelled within a week."

I see their point, but I press further. "So essentially it's moments of boredom that could be punctuated by sheer terror at any given moment?"

They look at each other again, then at me and reply in unison "Yeah. Pretty much."

I let that soak in for a second before I reply, "Yeah, screw that. I get jumpy when my microwave goes off when I'm waiting for a hot pocket. I can't imagine going from here to having to wrestle a meth head biker."

The salt and pepper cop then mimics me getting tossed around by a biker and fake-throws me over the counter holding the coffee like a bouncer tosses an unruly customer over the bar during a brawl. We're laughing and everyone within earshot is giving us strange looks.

I take a sip of my coffee and think, these guys are ok. They aren't too dissimilar from us civilians. I then recall the time I was let go by a cop with just a warning and asked, "Hey I've been pulled over and let go with just a warning. What gives? Is there a

Konami code or something that allows you to get unlimited breaks and works every time?"

The salt and pepper cop matter of factly says, "Just don't be a dick. Simple as that. Most times we can assess whether you're going to be a threat or are mentally ill or whatever, so if you are just a nice person and don't give us attitude and admit you messed up, chances are we'll let you go."

"Well that sounds simple enough." I say as I feel like I've just been given some secret tip that will allow me to blow stop signs for the rest of my life and avoid the repercussions.

The balding cop then says, "It isn't. This is our job, but do you really think we want to get out of the car to bust your balls? Do you want to do extra at your job?" he said to me with enough sincerity that he honestly wanted to know.

"Hell no! Cause I don't. No way. Bare minimum anymore."

"Exactly," he exclaims while raising his hand like this is a total no-brainer.

"If I'm out of my car then you did something wrong. Plain and simple. And yeah, we do get a shitty rap but most of us just want to finish the job and go home. "

His eyes trail off as if he's thinking about his couch or his wife or his kids, anything but this job. Then a call comes across his walkie-talkie. They put down their coffee and head towards the exit. Before they pass me the one cop says, "Also, sometimes some people just need a break." And with that they disappear out the door to their squad car. They turn on their lights and the sirens that pierce the store walls, to go save someone's day.

Workers

Every time I enter Wawa at noon I'm reminded that a half hour just isn't enough time for lunch. The mass amounts of people who flood this store during peak lunch rush are a testament to that fact. People are rushing around to and fro like contestants on some Wawa version of "Supermarket Sweep" and even though I was once told the goal is to get the customer in and out within 90 seconds, we all know what happens to the best laid plans. Sure, the store is laid out in a way that would support the 90 second theory, and it looks like the entire place is built for speed, but the person who once told me this fact also believes that 9/11 was an inside job, so I tend to take the things he says with a grain of salt. As I approach the line to the automated kiosk to order my Italian hoagie, I take a look around. I realize that whoever said, "if you have only a half hour for lunch, you have a job not a career" was so right. The very nature of our 21st century always-on-the-go economy means that we all have jobs now and you have to pull a Joey Chestnut and scarf that sandwich down if you want to get that **TPS** report in by 3 p.m.

The checkout line is a democratic amalgam of occupations that almost seems like a terrible joke a dad would tell at Thanksgiving dinner. Like castoffs thrown together at the rejects table at a wedding, we'd never be together in any other circumstances. I'm third in line, sandwiched between a young woman in her twenties dressed in a pantsuit ensemble and a very tall, and from what I can gather, former lacrosse player in an impeccably tailored suit who is yammering away on his Bluetooth.

I caught a quick glance of the woman's ID tag for work. In the picture, she's smiling, bright, bubbly, most likely on her first day of work. Now she's furiously slamming her fingers into her phone while sighing, as the corporate lacrosse guy is going back and forth between bragging about sleeping with two women at this job and the deal he just closed. I can't tell if her sighing is a reaction to her phone or to him. I assume from her stern look it's a mixture of both.

Currently occupying the ordering kiosk is an older gentleman, maybe in his mid-fifties, wearing paint-splattered work pants and the tattered sweatshirt of some contracting company. The various lines in his face make it resemble one of those old road maps that would be kept in a glove box. He winces in a way that people do when they are concentrating and want everyone in the room to be quiet and he jerks back when the Bluetooth guy screams "Ah-yo!" at the end of a double entendre.

I watch him push on the screen with all the hesitation in the world, like if he were to make a mistake he would have to start the whole thing over again. The same way I would try to precisely time a jump in Super Mario Brothers. It's almost like he knows his strength and his rough fingers might shatter the screen. He gently places each finger like he's booping the nose of his grandchild.

A hairnet-wearing deli worker screams out ,"Order number 666," and everyone in line and at the coffee station laughs. A diminutive grass-clippings-covered Latin American man bobs through the crowd to claim his order of soup and a buttered roll and deposits his ticket in the basket. He doesn't find the joke so funny.

As the old man continues to make love to the kiosk with his finger, the woman behind me begins to tap her foot to some rhythm that can only be described as nerve-wracking. Her hair is pulled back so far and tight that by looking at her it's impossible to gauge her emotions. If it wasn't for her tapping I wouldn't be sure what emotions she had, if any at all.

She's fierce and pretty in a way that I can't make eye contact with her for too long, or I'll feel every insecurity and botched prom invite come rushing to the surface. Instead I stare straight ahead and read the TV with the ads for iced coffee.

She abruptly stops tapping her foot and I feel a whoosh against my back as she can no longer wait and makes a break for the prepared sandwich and salad case. When she dives in to rummage through the salads, she bends over and I watch as two men in polo shirts and khakis nudge each other and whisper what I'm convinced is a lewd remark. I'm half certain that judging by her intensity, she either doesn't notice or doesn't care. I assume after working at a major corporation for years has either made her immune to the ham-handedness of bosses and their ass slaps or she has resigned herself to the fact that lurking deep inside every man is a pig. I kind of want her to see them pointing or maybe catch one of them saying something so she can throw a punch.

She settles on a salad, removes herself from the display and walks past the two men. She looks them dead in the eyes and says, "Hope you boys enjoyed the show" in a way that is reminiscent of a teacher scolding you for throwing a paper airplane, and less stripper asking if the bachelor party would like to have another table dance. A look of shame washes over their faces, and they don't allow their eyes to follow her to the end cap holding the Doritos.

I turn to see the contractor has finished his order and he's holding up his printed ticket as if he's studying a piece of microfiche containing state secrets. He steps out of the path of the hard-charging corporate type who is barreling in to order, while simultaneously filling the store with his jocularity that is so loud even the girl in pajamas scoffs.

And just before I am about to climb him as if he were the stairs to a tree house and yank the Bluetooth out of his head he finally hangs up. Then as he takes his place in front of the kiosk he turns to me and says, "You know they never tell you in law school about the awful people you'll have to converse with. Like some of the most awful people on the planet." I laugh with him because up until this moment, this is exactly what I was thinking about him.

"Yeah, well they aren't going to use that as a selling point on the brochure."

He nods while laughing as if he's picturing a life after reading an honest college advertisement.

"Don't worry about it," I say to him while still laughing. "I've had my share of awful conversations. I once broke up with a girl over the phone while I waited in line to buy smokes."

He laughs maniacally, in a way that reminds you of a villain in an eight-bit Nintendo game.
"I'm a lawyer," he says. "I've done all sorts of awful things, but man, that is savage as hell."

His utter look of amazement at what I consider to be my most awful act is confirmation enough that I probably won't have a seat next to the Lord in heaven.

His laughing trails and is replaced by a look of pensive confusion. "I mean they tell you to go to school. Get a good job so you can make tons of money. They should tell you how to be happy and have a good quality of life."

I immediately chime in, "Yeah but then capitalism would collapse and we'd all be fighting over these hoagies with ties wrapped around our heads."

He laughs and adjusts his belt that from the looks of it probably costs more than what I make in a week. It was probably made from the hide of a Waygu cow. His suit seems more like a prison than a reflection of his personal style and status. Suddenly, it just doesn't fit him as well anymore.

"Yeah," I reply after a brief pause, "They expect you to make the biggest decision of your life when you are at an age when you can barely decide whether you should go to the Dave Matthews or Rusted Root concert."

"Or getting laid, I mean that's all I thought about then."

I immediately shoot back, "And how did that work out for you?"

He smiles and says, "Well it turns out that women actually want someone to be present in the relationship, in both physical and the emotional sense. With the hours I keep and the fact that I'm almost always working when I'm at home, not well."

"Then what would you like to do?" I asked. And almost instantly he blurts out, "Become a plumber." It's as if this plumber fantasy is what keeps his soul alive during all the depositions and paperwork. It's the very thing that keeps him from punching a judge and lighting up his office with an automatic firearm.

His face becomes animated and alive, he goes on to explain how much he loves working with his hands and how his father was a plumber and it's good honest work. He likes fixing things. He's good at it. You can tell he'd rather discuss hot water heaters than constitutional or tort law any day. I let him finish and then I asked him, "Well why not quit and become a plumber?"

"It's easier said than done. I've got the career, the house, the car. I don't know, maybe someday I'll give it all up."

His number is called and he grabs his Panini and begins to walk away. I remember the dusty guitar in my room and how I planned on singing "Crash Into Me" to my high school sweetheart at our twenty year reunion last September and think, "Maybe not."

Weirdos

My number is called and I quickly grab my Italian hoagie and small side of macaroni and cheese because clearly there's an Italian theme to my lunch today. I turn around and suddenly, as if he materialized from some time-traveling wormhole, I slam right into a diminutive old man wearing an eye patch. He staggers, seemingly unalarmed that a stranger just bulldozed into him and exclaims, "What on earth did I come here for?" as if he quantum leaped into this Wawa. We don't exchange pleasantries, he just hobbles over towards the milk section as if to say, "Well I'm here. Might as well buy something."

Seeing him makes me think of all the strange and absurd characters I've come across over the years frequenting this store. There are so many and at all times you can find some oddity of the human condition, someone who just seems out of place like that one-eyed old man. It's as if the Wawa logo acts like the Bat signal for the deranged.

I'm sure to outsiders the very fact that people shop in their sleepwear or eat on top of a trashcan is absurd enough, but that is totally acceptable here and speaks to the utilitarian spirit of the store. Maybe that's why I didn't think twice when I once saw a man dressed like a pirate arguing with the guy making his sandwich because he didn't put enough meat on it. It was at 1 p.m. on a Tuesday in the middle of February.

I can hear the one-eyed man make all sorts of noises as he rummages through the milk display searching for God knows what. Probably an expiration date extension. I'm sure reading the small print on the milk carton proves difficult with one eye. Nobody else is even batting an eye at the man, pun intended. Somehow, we all know in our hearts this store is the perfect refuge, a phalanx to hide behind when the slings and arrows of life become a little too much to bear. A perfect refuge indeed. This store seems built for it. It's open 24 hours, has amazing prepared foods and a bathroom that I once saw a man shaving in at 2 a.m.

During a snowstorm, I once bore witness to two grown men in bikinis come in to buy condoms to satisfy some snow load drinking game dare. Another time, I was grabbed by the shoulders by an elderly disheveled man, his body smelling of urine and liquor. He screamed in my face: "I'm a veteran of the galactic war of freedom." All I could do was salute him. It's the least I could do for our veterans.

For the lost, the forgotten, the lonely, Wawa acts as a sort of "Cheers" in some regard. Now that some stores sell beer that is slowly becoming more of a reality. Every store has at least one resident odd duck customer, while some have several. The staff is often on a first name basis with them. With so much activity going on, said weirdos become lost in the comings and goings and sort of just melt into the display cases, just like another bag of Funyuns amongst a sea of Sun Chips.

I know where this store's resident weirdo is. He's always camped out by the newspaper section. He's got the front page of The Inquirer spread out before him facing the window like he's offering up a prayer from the police blotter to the Wawa gods above.

He's easily in his mid-sixties to early seventies but it's almost impossible to tell. I've never seen him wear anything but a stained gray trench coat with an equally grimy white shirt underneath. His pants are barely held up by a shoelace that he uses as a belt, and he walks around like a teenager with saggy jeans, holding up his pants with one hand. He's bald with some skin tags on his head, and his taped glasses perch off his nose precariously as if they are a suicidal jumper hanging off the railing of the Golden Gate Bridge. People navigate around him as I imagine grandchildren do to their grandfather who is in his La-Z-Boy reading the sports section.

His appearance reminds me of a rescued turtle and I try not to make fun of him, especially since I once parked next to his Dodge Neon, the inside of which resembled a Wawa graveyard with its copious amounts of used coffee cups and old newspapers.

A spry employee handing out free macchiato samples approaches him. She taps him on the shoulder and he greets her by name. She offers him one of the samples in the same manner a priest during the communion would offer the Host to a parishioner. He thanks her profusely and they engage in small talk.

I think maybe she's nice to him because he's alone and this is the only human interaction he'll get all day. Perhaps he just enjoys reading the paper in the middle of this hell that is the lunch rush. Maybe I shouldn't be staring so intently at him. Maybe he took the ferry here once and stayed on a bit too long. Maybe I should get a paper, see how the Phillies are doing. I look at my watch and realize I don't have enough time to read it and head towards the line.

Paying With Change Guy

As I make my way towards the checkout counter I'm reminded again that the goal Wawa is to get customers out of the store as quickly as humanly possible. It seems like the store is organized and staffed for this purpose, so that's why I always treat a trip here the same way I would treat a jewel heist, except I'm here for the Tastykakes, not the diamonds.

Is it possible to go from the sandwich kiosk, to the coffee station, to the chip aisle and then checked out in under 90 seconds? I don't know. 90 seconds can seem like the blink of an eye or an eternity, depending on who you run into while you're in there. It's all the fun of a NASCAR pit stop with only the occasional crash to break up the monotony. Imagine your sandwich and wares are the tires, and the people in there are the brick wall around turn two. I'm well over the allotted 90 second time, but I still feel pretty good as I make my way to the checkout counter. The entirety of my lunchtime hasn't been eaten away. Maybe this means I could qualify as a contestant on "Wawa

Sweep" but instead of collecting roasts and diapers, I collect hoagies and cigarettes and there's no happy ending.

As I'm racing to the finish line, I'm beaten out for the number one spot by a man in his forties. One by one behind me the line forms. The business woman with her salad and scowl, that weird old man appears behind her with some Wawa iced tea and Twizzlers, the patriarchal contractor behind him clutching his sandwich in his arms, and beyond him is the girl in pajamas, who again is screaming into her phone while her child destroys the candy display tucked under the checkout counter.

The ever-chipper cashier rings up the man's items and I marvel at the ballet of sandwich making and cashiers and how it runs with such precision. It's like a well-rehearsed production of "Swan Lake."

The man in front of me gets his total and he reaches in his pocket and pulls out an Everest-size mountain of change and the whole production grinds to a halt.

The woman behind me lets out a sigh so powerful that if my neck were a tree it would've been blown over. The old man adjusts his eye patch, seemingly more concerned with what universe he's currently in. The grizzled contractor gives a look like his son just told him he was gay. The girl in pajamas lets out an audible "What the hell!" with her Access card visible in her hand.

I stay silent. I've been that guy before. I know the feeling of shame that washes over you as the people in line begin to judge your entire existence. His clothes aren't tattered and he doesn't look homeless. He's not quite a J. Crew model but maybe he lost his job. Maybe his sick child wiped out his savings. Maybe he's recently divorced.

I just know that for years my superpower was the ability to cull enough change from my car and couch to buy a pack of smokes.

The cashier gives a tested look as if he's saying, "Why don't you have a damn debit card?" Like nobody in this line has ever been low on money and played a game of "Debit Card Roulette." The shame in his eyes becomes more palpable as each coin he lays down on the counter makes a noise like a pipe bomb ricocheting in an alley.

Although change is an acceptable form of currency, there is still a certain stigma attached to using it. It's as if using it makes you subhuman. How does paying for a loaf of bread with pennies and dimes strip you of your humanity? It doesn't, but the line behind me grows ever more agitated as the forces of the 21st century economy play out before their eyes.

The anger has reached its crescendo when finally a friendly voice breaks the tension by screaming, "Next in line please!" The tension dissipates as the line behind me rushes to the newly opened register.

The cashier finishes counting the coins and the man politely says to me, "I'm really sorry about that, man." I instinctively pat him on the back and say, "Hey man, I've been there. For years I used Coinstar as my official bank."

He laughs heartily and I'm not sure if it's out of relief or if he found my quip funny. The cashier hands him his bag and he quickly departs from the store.

Out The Same Way
You Came In

My transaction is quick and painless, and I've luckily won the roulette portion of this trip once again. As I head to the exit, I catch up with the customer before me who holds the door for me to leave. I hold the door for the incoming customer who is an older gentleman who could be a dead-ringer for Old Man Logan from the Wolverine comics. He in turn, holds the door for the young businesswoman exiting, who in turn holds the door for the outgoing contractor.

An angry pit bull is tied to the railing outside, a Cerberus guarding the point of exit and entry. A man in his thirties, dressed in denim with a Jack Nicholson haircut straight out of "The Shining" walks towards the cigarette disposal, opens it and begins to sift through the cigarette butts like he's an archaeologist hired by Marlboro to sift through an ancient tobacco-laden dig site. I approach him and offer him a few smokes from my pack. He readily accepts, then turns and walks off into the distance.

I pass the old men by the trash can. They give me a nod, I nod back out of respect. I overhear them saying something about the Marines, Afghanistan and Vietnam. I'm unable to make out the connection in the little time I have between passing them and getting to my truck.

I open my truck door. The sky is now a Mordor gray and raindrops splash upon my windshield. I take a sip of coffee and watch as the contractor with a ladder-laden truck almost backs into the businesswoman who lays on her horn with all the intense fury of a jilted lover.

He gives her the finger and takes off. I watch as she transforms into the Muppet Animal. All arms flailing about but with f-words flying.

"You've got to be kidding me! He's still here?" I scream as I see Charon the Ferryman out of the side of my eye working his game on another unsuspecting victim. I turn the key to the ignition of my mail truck and pull away. Pleased once again by another trip to Wawa.

*The following coupons are for entertainment purposes only

$2.00 ON

Gargoyles of Wawa Membership®

This coupon is good for an additional $2.00 on to the annual membership price to the Gargoyles of Wawa® club. This is a yearly license that allows for standing and loitering at any Wawa trashcan at anytime. Members must heed way to Wawa employees when cleaning outside and changing bags, and to all Wawa delivery trucks and drivers. Present this coupon to the scruffiest person standing around a Wawa trashcan at anytime, though you should be mindful before interrupting any good stories that may be in progress. This membership grants all members the ability to use the trashcan for its intended and unintended purposes. Usage is limited by members on site using trashcan before you. Trashcan hierarchy is claimed in order members arrive and disperse. Gargoyles of Wawa® membership will be revoked if you are ever accused or guilty of purchasing or distributing cigarettes or beer for minors.

Wawa

UP TO 99¢ OFF

Coupon must be presented before checkout. This is good for one use to make exact change of a cash transaction using the overflowing charity change found outside the collection box at any register. No more than $0.99 in change can be used. Coupon may not be used for purchases under $1.00, as an attempt to make a free transaction. Any change found inside the box is not eligible. Boxes must not be tampered with. Only 1 coupon valid per person. It's okay, take the overflowing change. There's enough in that box and all the boxes in all the Wawa stores to open a brand new Wawa store. No one will notice. And if they do, this coupon makes it okay for one time and one time only.

Wawa

FREE

1 Pack of Soup Crackers

No purchase necessary. This coupon is good for 1 FREE pack of soup crackers. Present this coupon to no one. Just take the crackers. They're free. Though in the event of a tie for the last pack of crackers, ties go to the customer that purchased soup. If in a tie with another coupon holder, determine who likes mayonnaise and they can take a pack of that instead. If neither like mayonnaise, then the crackers must be opened and shared. If more than 2 coupon holders are in a tie for the last pack of crackers, the first two must share and any others can then claim a mayonnaise packet or a free courtesy cup of water.

Wawa

THANK YOU

The following people were instrumental in making this book a reality. Ben Fidler (Toxic), Chris Scamuffa, Rick Helpa, Pat House, Pat and Vickie Graves, Steve Rees, Jen Cleary, Mike Rainey, Susan Lynch, Dave Kupsey, Dan Kupsey, Jim Breslin and everyone within the Philadelphia comedy community for being some of the best human beings I've ever met. And thank you to you for buying this. I love you all.

For Bill and Cenzo.

Made in the USA
San Bernardino, CA
09 November 2017